AF413629
To ________________
From ________________
on ________________

THE SPARROW

WHO FELL TO THE GROUND

ANTHONY DeSTEFANO   ILLUSTRATED BY RICHARD COWDREY

SOPHIA INSTITUTE PRESS
Manchester, NH

This book is for my brother, Judge Vito M. DeStefano.

—Anthony DeStefano

To Anthony DeStefano — the author of this and so many other stories — whose foundation and inspiration is the Word of God. Anthony's desire has always been to spark children's curiosity and creativity through lyrical storytelling, and to captivate their minds with visuals that point to the timeless truths of our Creator. Thank you, Anthony, for choosing me to walk beside you in telling these stories.

—Richard Cowdrey

SOPHIA
INSTITUTE PRESS

Sophia Institute Press®
Box 5284, Manchester, NH 03108
1-800-888-9344

www.SophiaInstitute.com
Sophia Institute Press® is a registered trademark of Sophia Institute.

print ISBN: 979-8-88911-404-8
eBook ISBN: 979-8-88911-405-5

Library of Congress Control Number: 2025943737

First printing, 2025

From the Bible

Are not two sparrows sold for a penny? Yet not one of them will fall to the ground outside your Father's care. And even the very hairs of your head are all numbered. So don't be afraid; you are worth more than many sparrows.

Matthew 10:29–31 (NIV)

There once was a place called the Valley of Tears
Where it rained and it poured for hundreds of years.

Deep in this valley on a rocky plateau,
There lived a small sparrow a long time ago.

This sparrow was born
with a broken right wing,
Which he kept all his life
in a little white sling.

Whenever the sparrow attempted to fly,
He'd get very weak and fall from the sky.

Down he would go, SPLATTER and SMASH!
The sparrow would slam to the ground with a CRASH!

Sad and ashamed, he wanted to cry.
How could a sparrow be frightened to fly?

Despite all his heartbreak and worries and fears,
He HAD to get out of the Valley of Tears.

The valley was scary when storms would come through.
The rains rarely stopped; the winds always blew.

Lightning would flash, and thunder would boom.
The days were so dreary, the nights full of gloom.

And yet there were times the clouds disappeared.
The downpours would stop, and everything cleared.

During those days the sparrow would see
Just how delightful the valley could be.

There in the heavens, shining so bright,
The sun would arise—a glorious sight!

The sun gave the sparrow a glimmer of hope.
Maybe he somehow could fly up the slope!

Over the mountain and out of the rain,
There might be less sorrow and suffering and pain.

He got so excited, he took off his sling.
Throwing it down, he freed his right wing.

He furrowed his brow and said a short prayer,
Then ran to the cliff and leaped in the air!

But just as he rose, he started to stall.
He hung in the air, then started to fall.

Dropping and whooshing,
he plummeted down,
BOINKING his beak
when he hit the hard ground.

"Oh no!" cried the sparrow. "I'm doing this wrong!
I must find a way to make my wing strong."

He spotted a twig; then, using some string,
He wrapped it around his broken right wing.

Then running and flapping with all of his might,
He jumped off the cliff and started his flight.

At first it felt pleasant to glide through the air.
His wing didn't hurt; the weather was fair.

The freedom of flying was good for his soul.
He even tried doing a loop and a roll.

But just at that moment, the sky turned to black.
A lightning bolt thundered and rumbled and cracked!

The wind shrieked and groaned; the rains pounded down;
the gusts tossed and shook the small sparrow around.

He heard his wing snap, then felt himself drop.
He crashed in a puddle, KERSPLASH and KERPLOP!

But there he encountered a shocking surprise:
A slithering snake and rats with red eyes!

Retying the twig, he tried to move fast.
He flapped his wings swiftly and took off at last.

But flying and crashing had made his wing sore.
The ache that he felt was hard to ignore.

He wanted to quit; he wanted to land.
The pain was too much for the bird to withstand.

Above him some vultures were circling around.
They hoped the small sparrow would fall to the ground.

The tears from the clouds came down without end.
The sparrow tried saying a prayer once again:

"God, help me escape this terrible storm
And get me to someplace that's sunny and warm.
Those vultures will eat me if I give up now.
I need to keep flapping and flying somehow."

High in the heavens, the moon shone its light.
The snow on the mountaintop gleamed frosty white.

Although he felt tired and worn out and weak,
The sparrow continued to fly toward the peak.

His feathers were drenched; his wing needed care.
The wounded bird seemed to be limping in air.

Upward he climbed; higher he flew.
The top of the mountain at last was in view!

Huffing and puffing, refusing to stop,
He finally made it up over the top!

Crossing the ridge, the bird was in awe
Of all the magnificent things that he saw:

Flowers and rivers and meadows and trees,
Sunshine and cities and vineyards and seas!

But all of a sudden, he heard a loud CRACK!
His broken wing crumpled and went very slack.

Down the bird tumbled: SWISH, WHISTLE, ZOOM!
He dropped like a rock: CLUNK, CLATTER, BOOM!

Swish
Whistle
Zoom!!

Shaking his head, he got to his feet.
He took a deep breath and smelled something sweet.
The smell came from lilies that rose from the ground —
Thousands of lilies that grew all around.

The bird stumbled forward while clutching his wing.
It felt torn and mangled and started to sting.

He came to a garden, lush and serene,
With trees full of flowers and grass, emerald green.

The garden was filled with animals too:
A bunny, a sheep, a bird that was blue;
An ox and a camel and donkeys were there—
There seemed to be all kinds of life everywhere.

Off in the corner he spotted a boy
Planting some seeds and smiling with joy.

The boy saw the sparrow, and turning his head,
He called out to him and quietly said:

"I see that you're hurting. Come over here.
Stretch out your wing; there's no need to fear."

Touching it lightly, he felt for the base.
Then moving it slowly, he put it in place.

And forming a cross
with two sticks of wood,
He fastened it gently
until it felt good.

"Your wing will mend fast
with the splint that I've made.
You see," said the boy,
"I'm a carpenter by trade."

In no time at all, the sparrow had healed,
There by the lilies that grew in the field.

The days overflowed with playing and fun.
But mostly he cherished the light from the sun.

Soon he was soaring and flying above,
Happy to be in this land full of love.

Yes, he had suffered for many a year,
But all of his suffering had led him to here.

The sparrow was grateful he fell to the ground.
He'd been lost in the valley—but now he was found.